Spicy

FRAGRANT WAYS
WITH EXOTIC HERBS AND SPICES.

ALAN HAYES

Angus&Robertson
An imprint of HarperCollins*Publishers*

CONTENTS

History and Traditions

SWEET SPICES, DRIED CITRUS PEEL, AROMATIC WOODS AND RICHLY FRAGRANT AND EXOTIC GUMS HAVE BEEN USED SINCE ANCIENT TIMES TO ENHANCE AND PRESERVE THE SCENTS OF DRIED FLOWERS AND HERBS. THEY PROVIDE A HINT OF EXOTIC MYSTERY, GIVING SUBTLE UNDERTONES TO SIMPLE FLOWER FRAGRANCES WITHOUT MASKING THEM.

The spice trade reaches back before recorded history. Archaeologists estimate that, by 50,000 BC, our ancestors were using aromatic spices to make food taste better. From the hieroglyphics on the walls of Egyptian pyramids, and from the Bible, we know that herbs and spices played vital roles in people's lives and finances in these times. Caravans with as many as 4000 camels travelled the trade routes of antiquity, carrying spices from the Orient, Calicut, and Goa to the markets in Nineveh, and Babylon. The road from Gilead to Egypt was part of the 'golden road to Samarkand', so named for its rich trade in pepper and cloves from India, cinnamon and nutmeg from the Spice Islands, and ginger from China.

The importance of spices in early times becomes easier to understand when we realise they were the only way in which food could be preserved. In the absence of refrigeration, the meat and game was often tainted and required rich spicy sauces to disguise the unpleasant flavour. Spices were also used singly or in combination to make fragrant burned and dried perfumes. These aromatic combinations are still enjoyed in today's favourite zesty scents, which often feature cinnamon, sandalwood, cedar and cloves; all those marvellous spices that our noses automatically associate with the Far East and the legendary tales of the Arabian Nights.

As in centuries past, rich and spicy exotic scents can enhance our lives. Of course it is possible to buy products from the supermarket; but it is much more rewarding to create a few special recipes of your own. In this book, you will find practical instructions for making gentle and refreshing cosmetics for skin and hair; simple remedies for common ailments; delicious and easy recipes for zesty food and summer drinks or warming winter toddies; and natural products to clean and perfume the home. Not only will they be a joy to use, they are also simple and creative gifts.

Spices

Spices should be bought and used whole for most fragrant mixtures, since their aroma begins to change and diminish from the moment they are ground. Whole spices will keep their aromas locked in, so they can be bought in fairly large quantities and then stored in airtight containers for up to two years. If you are making potpourri, it is worth keeping aside a few whole cloves or small pieces of whole mace or cinnamon stick to decorate the mixture when finished.

Unless a particular recipe calls for spices to be ground into a fine powder, they are best coarsely crushed with a mortar and pestle. Some, such as nutmeg, can be grated.

Some successful spice combinations are:

* CINNAMON, CASSIA, CLOVES, MACE
* CINNAMON, ALLSPICE, CLOVES, MACE
* CARDAMOM, CORIANDER, ANISE, CARAWAY
* CLOVES, ALLSPICE, MACE, CASSIA

8

SPICY

Woods

Scented woods combine well with other ingredients and are most appealing to the senses. They are available as chips or raspings and should be bought in small amounts and stored in airtight jars or sealed packets away from hot sun.

Those most commonly available are:

SANDALWOOD	SHARP AND BITTER SCENT
CEDAR	PINE-LIKE FRAGRANCE
SASSAFRAS	SPICY

Dried Citrus Peel

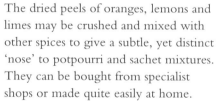

The dried peels of oranges, lemons and limes may be crushed and mixed with other spices to give a subtle, yet distinct 'nose' to potpourri and sachet mixtures. They can be bought from specialist shops or made quite easily at home.

Thinly pare the skin, making sure that no pith is left attached to it (otherwise the peel may go mouldy) and place in the sun until completely dried. Next, stud the peel with cloves and dry in a warm oven (100°C/212°F) until crisp. Remove peel and reduce it to a powder with a mortar and pestle or in a blender.

Gums

Gums are the dried, scented resins of certain trees, most of which come from the Far East. They are available in both crystal and powder form. Unlike spices, they are less aromatic in their whole form and must be crushed in a mortar and pestle to fully release their fragrance. Keep them all in airtight jars or packets.

The gums most readily available and commonly used are:

* **GUM BENZOIN**
* **FRANKINCENSE**
* **MYRRH**
* **MUSK**

Equipment

When making these recipes you will only need basic kitchen equipment, and a few other odds and ends that you will probably also have in your kitchen. However, before you start there are a number of precautions you should take so as not to contaminate or mar the preparations:

✴ Always use distilled water in the recipes, as tap water contains chemicals and impurities. This is essential, because contaminated water may interfere with the action of the ingredients.

✴ Do not use aluminium, metal or non-stick pans for boiling or steeping, or for the preparation of recipes. They may chemically react with the natural ingredients. Use only stainless steel or enamel pans for boiling and ceramic or glass pots for steeping.

✴ All equipment must be kept scrupulously clean, and preferably used only for the preparation of herbal recipes. This safeguards them from contamination by foodstuffs and other foreign substances. Again, do not use metal or aluminium utensils; always use a wooden spoon to stir.

✴ Sterilise all the containers and lids you intend to store your creams or herbal waters in.

✴ Label everything you make: don't rely on your memory.

Around

Pomanders

POMANDERS ARE EASY TO MAKE AND A JOY TO HAVE
AROUND THE HOME. THIS SWEET LIME POMANDER WILL
FILL A ROOM OR CUPBOARD WITH ITS RICH, SPICY
FRAGRANCE.

Sweet Lime Pomander

1 LARGE LIME
25 G (1 OZ) CLOVES
½ TABLESPOON ORRIS ROOT POWDER
½ TABLESPOON GROUND CORIANDER
½ TABLESPOON GROUND CARDAMOM
½ TABLESPOON GROUND CINNAMON
3 DROPS LIME OIL

Gently knead the lime in your hands to soften the skin. Make a ring of holes in it with a wooden skewer or darning needle, and press a clove into each hole. Be very careful to just pierce the outer skin, not go right through. Continue to do this, working in circles towards each end, until the entire lime is covered. If a ribbon is to be tied around the finished pomander, leave a central cross shape round the lime, the width of your chosen ribbon, free from cloves.

Mix together the ground spices and orris root powder, then add the essential oil of lime, mixing in well. Roll the lime around in the mixture. Pat it in well with your fingers. Wrap the lime in tissue paper, put it in a brown paper bag, and leave it in a dry, dark, airy place for 3 to 5 weeks to cure. During this time the lime will dry out completely and shrink. Your pomander is now ready for use.

If you have left a cross for the ribbon, tie it around your pomander and leave a loop about 15 cm (6 in) on top for hanging it by. Velvet ribbon looks especially nice. Otherwise, put the lime pomander in a small net bag and hang it up in that.

Perfumed Room Sprays

EXPERIMENT WITH DIFFERENT COMBINATIONS OF
ESSENTIAL OILS TO CREATE DIFFERENT SCENTS:
PERHAPS A CLEAN LEMON-SCENTED SPRAY FOR AN
INVALID'S ROOM, OR A MELLOW SPICY AROMA TO GIVE
YOUR HOME A LOVELY RELAXED ATMOSPHERE.

Spicy Nutmeg Spray

This is a delightfully fragrant blend of essential oils with a subtle hint of nutmeg. As a bonus, it also has quite potent antibacterial and antiviral properties, making it very useful when illness is around.

16 DROPS OIL OF CHAMOMILE
8 DROPS OIL OF LAVENDER
8 DROPS OIL OF YLANG YLANG
16 DROPS OIL OF JASMINE
60 DROPS (1.5 ML) OIL OF BERGAMOT
40 DROPS (1 ML) OIL OF NUTMEG
10 ML (⅓ FL OZ) VODKA
500 ML (16 FL OZ) DISTILLED WATER

Dissolve the oils in the vodka and mix thoroughly with the distilled water. Store in a pump-spray bottle and use on a fine mist setting.

Incense

IN ANCIENT TIMES SWEET SPICES, SUCH AS CINNAMON, CASSIA, CLOVES, ALLSPICE AND NUTMEG, WERE MIXED WITH HERBS AND BURNT TO PERFUME THE AIR WITH AN ENJOYABLE SWEETNESS. IT WAS ALSO THOUGHT THAT THEY WOULD KEEP AWAY INFECTION. THESE MIXTURES WERE LATER BLENDED WITH GUMS AND OTHER AROMATICS AND BECAME THE FORERUNNER OF THE INCENSE STICKS WE BURN TODAY.

SPICY

Strongly Scented Incense

The following recipe is for easy-to-make incense cones that will fill your home with an exotic, yet mysterious aroma.

SPICE MIXTURE
2 DROPS LEMON OIL
2 DROPS NUTMEG OIL
2 DROPS ROSE OIL
COMBINE EQUAL QUANTITIES OF:
CRUSHED CINNAMON
CRUSHED NUTMEG
MINCED VANILLA POD
CRUSHED ALLSPICE

DRIED LEMON PEEL
DRIED LEMON VERBENA
DRIED LAVENDER
DRIED ROSEMARY
WITH:
2 TABLESPOONS VERY FINE SAWDUST
2 TEASPOONS GUM ARABIC
40 ML (1½ FL OZ) WATER

Reduce the spice mixture (including oils) to a powder
by rubbing through a fine wire sieve. Mix thoroughly
together. (Excess mixture can be stored in an airtight
jar for future use.)

Thoroughly mix together the sawdust and
2 tablespoons of the spice mixture, then add the water,
in which the gum arabic has been dissolved. When all
ingredients are well mixed, shape into cones and allow
to dry.

Place cones on small metal dishes, or other suitable
objects, and light: the incense will slowly smoulder,
filling the room with its fragrance. Special metal and
ceramic incense burners are available in health food
shops and some chemists or gift shops.

Sachets

ACCORDING TO THE ARABIAN NIGHTS, CORIANDER WAS
ONE OF THE INGREDIENTS USED OFTEN IN LOVE
POTIONS. PERHAPS THIS IS WHY CORIANDER SEEDS
HAVE BEEN USED THROUGH THE CENTURIES FOR
CLEANSING AND BEAUTIFYING THE SKIN. WITH THEIR
STRONG, SPICY AROMA, CORIANDER SEEDS ALSO MAKE
A FRAGRANT ADDITION TO A BASIC POTPOURRI
MIXTURE.

Coriander Sachet

A simple recipe which will keep your wardrobe free of musty smells and tease your senses each time you open the door. It is a particularly good blend to use near a man's suits, which can tend to smell stale.

1 CUP CORIANDER SEEDS, LIGHTLY CRUSHED
1 CUP DRIED ROSE PETALS
DRIED PEEL OF 1 ORANGE
10 WHOLE CLOVES
2 TABLESPOONS ORRIS ROOT POWDER

Blend all ingredients together in a ceramic bowl, using your hands to ensure a good mix. Finely crumble rose petals, but do not reduce them to a powder. Put into small cotton or silk sachets and hang along the coathanger rail. Natural fibres are best for sachets as they enable the herbs and spices to breathe and release their perfumes. Do not fill sachets too full. Pack them fairly loosely and the mixture will release its fragrance more easily.

Scented Woods

WOOD CAN BE SIMPLY IMPREGNATED WITH SPICY OR
TANGY ESSENTIAL OILS TO PRODUCE A LONG-LASTING
SOURCE OF FRAGRANCE IN YOUR HOME. KEEP PIECES
OF SCENTED WOOD IN DRAWERS OR SCATTER THEM
ALONG SHELVES IN THE LINEN PRESS TO KEEP SHEETS
AND TOWELS SMELLING FRESH.

Any pieces of dried wood or dried wood shavings can be used, as they will easily soak up essential oils. Use your imagination to create something really different and attractive, perhaps a piece of interesting driftwood or small branches. Not only will they be visually impressive, but they will be aromatically satisfying, too.

To impregnate your wood with fragrance, add a chosen essential oil to a container of water until it is sufficiently scented, then let the wood soak in this. For a subtle colour you might like to add a few drops of an appropriate food dye.

Choose from any of the following spice oils to suit your mood or surroundings:

RELAXING	STIMULATING	ROMANTIC
SANDALWOOD	MANDARIN	BENZOIN
FRANKINCENSE	CORIANDER	PATCHOULI

Potpourri

THE LITERAL AND RATHER UNROMANTIC TRANSLATION OF THE FRENCH NAME *POT POURRI* IS 'ROTTEN POT', A REFERENCE TO THE OLD 'MOIST' WAY OF MAKING IT WHERE THE FLOWER PETALS AND LEAVES WERE LEFT TO ROT DOWN AND FERMENT.

The 'dry' method of making potpourri is the more usual nowadays — simply place any mixtures of flowers and herbs in pots or bowls to fill a room with scent. Adding exotic essential oils and spices can create a sensual and romantic atmosphere, *Arabian Nights* style.

Oriental Sweet Jar

25 G (1 OZ) DRIED BASIL
25 G (1 OZ) CASSIA BARK
25 G (1 OZ) CRUSHED CORIANDER
25 G (1 OZ) CRUSHED CARDAMOM SEEDS
25 G (1 OZ) POWDERED ORANGE RIND
15 G (½ OZ) ORRIS ROOT POWDER
4 DROPS LEMON OIL
2 DROPS BASIL OIL

In a ceramic bowl mix all the ingredients together,
except the essential oils, using your hands to ensure a
good mix. Add the essential oils a drop at a time,
mixing in well after each drop and testing for scent.
Add more if the scent is not strong enough.

Put the potpourri in a plastic bag and seal. Leave it
to cure in a dry, dark spot for 6 weeks, giving the mix
a good shake every other day.

SPICY

Display your potpourri in a tightly-sealed, attractive glass jar, away from direct sunlight. Open the container each day for about an hour to allow the fragrance to waft around the room. You will find that the scent will last for hours. Note that although potpourri may look very attractive displayed in an open bowl, its fragrance will not last as well.

Refresh your potpourri once a week with one or two drops of the essential oils, always testing the scent before adding more. The oils are made from the same range of scented plants, but the strength and availability of the different brands can vary.

Furniture Polish

IMAGINE YOUR LOUNGE AND DINING ROOMS EXUDING THE SUBTLE, YET DISTINCTIVE SCENT OF SPICE, OR THE REFRESHING, CLEAN FRAGRANCE OF PINE.

This old–fashioned furniture cream will leave timber furniture and surfaces smelling wonderfully aromatic, as well as bringing them to a brilliant shine.

125 ML (4 FL OZ) DISTILLED WATER
125 G (4 OZ) BEESWAX
25 G (1 OZ) PURE SOAP FLAKES
500 ML (16 FL OZ) NATURAL TURPENTINE
1 TEASPOON ESSENTIAL OIL OF EITHER
CEDARWOOD, CYPRESS, OR SANDALWOOD

Put the distilled water in an enamel pan and heat to boiling point. Reduce to a simmer, add the soapflakes, and stir continuously until they are dissolved. Remove from heat.

Melt the wax in a double saucepan over a medium heat.

When it is completely liquid add the remaining ingredients, except the essential oil, and stir until dissolved and blended. Remove from heat and pour into a ceramic bowl. Add the essential oil and beat until cool and texture is creamy.

Store in a suitable wide-mouthed container with a tight-fitting lid.

Spice Ropes

THERE IS LITTLE ROMANTIC LORE SURROUNDING THE USE OF SPICE ROPES. THEY ARE, IN FACT, AN EXTREMELY POPULAR INVENTION OF OUR MODERN CIVILISATION. SPICE ROPES ARE MADE BY PLAITING LENGTHS OF THICK WOOL OR ROUGH, NATURAL FIBRE ROPE TOGETHER, LEAVING ONE END FRAYED AND SECURING THE OTHER TO A WOODEN RING FOR HANGING. LITTLE BAGS OF COLOURED COTTON MATERIAL FILLED WITH A SPICY MIX ARE THEN TIED AT INTERVALS ALONG THE ROPE, TOGETHER WITH TINY BUNCHES OF DRIED FLOWERS OR CINNAMON STICKS.

Spice ropes can be placed in any room in the house, but are particularly suitable for hanging in pantries or beside the stove where the warmth will accentuate their scent.

2 TABLESPOONS GROUND CINNAMON
2 TABLESPOONS ORRIS ROOT POWDER
2 TABLESPOONS GROUND CLOVES
4 DROPS CLOVE OIL
2 TABLESPOONS GROUND NUTMEG
4 DROPS ORANGE OIL
(MAKES ENOUGH FOR 2 ROPES)

Mix the spices and orris root powder together in a ceramic bowl, using your hands to ensure a good mix. Add the oils, a drop at a time, mixing well and testing the scent after each addition. Place in a plastic bag and seal tightly. Leave in a dry, dark spot for 6 weeks to mature, and give the mix a good shake every other day.

To make the spice bags, cut small squares of cotton material and place a heaped teaspoon of the mixture in the centre of each one. Gather up the sides and secure with coloured wool or string, then attach the bags at intervals along the rope. Decorate all the space remaining, tying on your choice of any of the following: cinnamon sticks, mace blades, whole star anise or whole nutmegs.

The scent of the rope should remain strong for about a year. Revive it by adding 2 drops of either clove or orange oil, or one drop of each, to the mixture in the bags.

Scented Candles

THESE SANDALWOOD AND PATCHOULI OIL CANDLES
WILL FRESHEN AND DELICATELY PERFUME STALE AIR,
LEAVING YOUR HOME WITH AN ALLURING AND
MYSTERIOUS FRAGRANCE.

350 G (11½ OZ) BEESWAX
12 DROPS SANDALWOOD OIL
6 DROPS PATCHOULI OIL

Melt the wax in a double boiler over a medium heat.
When completely liquid remove from heat and add
essential oils, one drop at a time, until mixture is
sufficiently scented to your taste. Then pour into
moulds.

Eucalyptus Candles

Lighting one of these aromatic candles in a room will
help to repel insects, as well as making the room smell
clean and fresh.

Melt sufficient beeswax in a double pan over a
medium heat, so that it does not burn. When
completely liquid add 20 ml (⅔ fl oz) eucalyptus oil to
every 500 ml (16 fl oz) wax. Pour into moulds and
allow to harden for 3 to 4 hours before using. Trim
the wick to 1 cm (½ in) and smooth the sides with a
cotton ball dipped in vegetable oil.

Wick

As a general guide, the bigger the candle the bigger the wick should be. If it is too small the melted wax will flood the flame and drip down the candle.

Wicks can be obtained from craft shops and hobby stores.

Wax

Beeswax is a high quality natural ingredient that gives good light, texture and colour. It is available from craft shops, but is less expensive if you can obtain it from a beekeeper in your area. Check your telephone book to contact the local beekeeping (or apiary) society.

Moulds

Moulds can be made from almost anything, such as small, attractive ceramic bowls or glass jars. Secure the wick in the bottom of the mould with a piece of plasticine, and then secure the other end to a pencil laid across its top. Remove the plasticine once the wax cools and shrinks.

Insect Repellent Pastilles

PROFESSIONAL PERFUMERS WERE ONCE EMPLOYED TO SCENT THE OFTEN MUSTY HOMES AND CASTLES OF YESTERYEAR. THE MOST COMMON METHOD WAS TO BURN SCENTED GUMS AND SPICES IN A CHAFING DISH WHICH WAS CARRIED FROM ROOM TO ROOM. THIS, IN TURN, GAVE RISE TO MANY RECIPES FOR INCENSE AND FOR PASTILLES TO FRESHEN THE HOME AND KEEP AWAY INFECTION.

Citronella Insect Repellent

These tiny aromatic pastilles smell delightfully fresh as they are burnt. They will also keep insects from annoying you, so they are ideal to use when entertaining out of doors.

30 G (1 OZ) BEESWAX
1 TABLESPOON EUCALYPTUS OIL
1 TEASPOON CITRONELLA OIL
½ TEASPOON OIL OF CLOVES

Melt the wax in a double saucepan over a medium heat until completely liquid. Remove from heat, add oils and pour a 1 cm (¼ in) layer into paper cup-cake cases.

When the wax hardens, but is still soft and pliable, shape into tiny balls. Pierce a hole in each one with a hot needle. Thread with a candle wick thick enough to ensure a snug fit. Trim one end flush and seal by warming the wax and smearing over the wick.

Place pastilles on small metal or ceramic dishes before lighting.

Exotic

HERBS & SPICES

Desserts

TANGY HERBS AND SPICES HAVE BEEN USED FOR
CULINARY PURPOSES SINCE THE MIDDLE AGES. LEMON
BALM WAS ONCE USED TO FLAVOUR AND CLARIFY WINE
AND ALE, AS WELL AS TO COMPLEMENT FRUIT,
CUSTARDS AND SAUCES WITH ITS SLIGHTLY TART
FLAVOUR. CINNAMON, WITH ITS SOFT SPICY SCENT AND
TASTE, HAS LONG BEEN VALUED AS A FLAVOURING IN
BOTH SWEET AND SAVOURY DISHES.

Lemon Balm Ice Cream

A delicious tangy treat that makes an excellent summer
dessert for all the family to enjoy.

150 ML (5 FL OZ) DOUBLE CREAM
150 ML (5 FL OZ) MILK
50 G (1 ⅓ OZ) SUGAR
2 EGG YOLKS, BEATEN
½ TEASPOON VANILLA ESSENCE
**1 TEASPOON FRESHLY CHOPPED LEMON VERBENA
LEAVES**

Partially beat the cream. Heat the milk and sugar then
pour into egg yolks, stirring constantly to make a
custard. Reheat very slowly, stirring constantly until

the mixture becomes thick—too much heat too soon will curdle it. Strain, add the vanilla and allow to cool.

Fold in the lemon verbena leaves and partially-whipped cream. Pour into a suitable tray and freeze.

Citrus Sorbet

This delicious citrus-flavoured frozen dessert is a wonderful finale to lunch on a hot summer's day. Its refreshing taste will leave your palate cool and tingling.

600 ML (20 FL OZ) WATER
150 G (5 OZ) SUGAR
2 DROPS LEMON ESSENTIAL OIL
2 DROPS GRAPEFRUIT ESSENTIAL OIL
2 DROPS LIME ESSENTIAL OIL
1 EGG WHITE
GRAPEFRUIT PULP, IF DESIRED

Boil the water, sugar and essential oils for 10 minutes. Cool, then partially freeze. Beat the mixture until it is soft and mushy. Beat the egg white until it is stiff. Add grapefruit pulp (optional) and fold in the egg white. Spoon into individual serving bowls and refreeze for 4 hours.

Spiced Apples

This is a delicious, spicy preserve which marries well with both sweet and savoury dishes. Serve it as a relish with cold meat and salads, or as a scrumptious dessert, topped off with yoghurt, or, use it as a mouth-watering, zesty filling for an apple pie.

6 LARGE GRANNY SMITH APPLES
500 G (16 OZ) SUGAR
2 CUPS (500 ML/16 FL OZ) WATER
RIND OF 1 LEMON
2 TEASPOONS WHOLE CLOVES
8 CORIANDER SEEDS
1 CINNAMON STICK, BROKEN
1 WHOLE VANILLA BEAN

SPICY

Peel, core and slice apples. Microwave or steam until just cooked (not mushy). Dissolve sugar in water over a low heat. Add remaining ingredients. Bring to the boil, reduce heat and simmer for 6 to 8 minutes.

Carefully place cooked apples in warm sterile jars. Strain syrup, reserving some of the whole spices, and pour carefully over apples. Add some of the spices to the apples and syrup. Seal while hot. When cool, label and date.

Lemon Pepper

A simple delicious and zesty substitute for conventional pepper. Lemon pepper gives an unusual, yet tantalising taste to fish and salad dishes.

50 G (1 ⅓ OZ) COARSELY GROUND BLACK PEPPERCORNS
4 DROPS OIL OF LEMON

Put pepper in a small glass jar. Add essential oil of lemon, mix together with a wooden stirrer, seal and leave for 3 days before use.

Add to a pepper mill with a fine grind and use as required.

Other tangy and interesting flavours can be obtained by substituting grapefruit or lime for the lemon oil. Never grind peppercorns until just before you use them as they quickly lose their strength when broken.

Drinks

Cinnamon Tea

A delicious, spicy tea that can be enjoyed morning or night as a refreshing alternative to conventional tea. It is a good natural remedy when recuperating after a long illness.

250 G (8 OZ) WHITE CLOVER BLOSSOMS
1 LARGE CINNAMON STICK, BROKEN INTO PIECES
1 TEASPOON FINELY GRATED ORANGE RIND
500 ML (16 FL OZ) BOILING WATER

Put the clover blossoms and cinnamon in an enamel pan and add boiling water. Bring to a simmer, add orange rind and cook gently for 5 minutes. Remove from heat, cover, and infuse for a further 5 minutes. Strain and sweeten to taste with honey.

Any excess tea may be stored in the refrigerator for up to 3 days and warmed before drinking.

Balm Brandy

One of the simplest ways to flavour alcoholic drinks is by steeping. Aromatic herbs and spices have been added to fortified wines and spirits since the 12th century. In fact they were often regarded as medicines because of their warming and stimulating effect.

This is a delicious, spicy drink that is excellent served as a liqueur. It is especially nice on cold winter nights, when it will give you an all-over warming glow.

1 SMALL HANDFUL FRESH LEMON BALM LEAVES
300 ML (10 FL OZ) BRANDY
1 DROP CORIANDER OIL
125 G (4 OZ) CLEAR HONEY
1 DROP CINNAMON OIL

Wash and bruise the lemon balm leaves and place them in the brandy. Leave to steep in a warm spot for 2 days, then strain through clean muslin, squeezing all liquid from the herbs. Add the honey, stirring well to dissolve; add the essential oils then bottle and seal.

Allow to stand for a week before using, so the taste and fragrance can mature.

Fragrant

BEAUTY

Cologne

FRAGRANT TOILET WATERS, OR 'SWETE WASHYNGE
WATERS', FIRST APPEARED IN PERSIA IN THE 10TH
CENTURY. DURING NORMAN TIMES, SUCH WATERS
WERE VERY WIDELY USED, FOR CLEANSING THE FACE
AND BODY, RINSING THE FINGERS BETWEEN COURSES
OF A MEAL AND FOR SCATTERING AROUND MUSTY-
SMELLING CHAMBERS.

It is a simple matter to infuse scented herbs and
spices in water and then strain the liquid before adding
it to your bath or using it in home-made cosmetics to
cleanse, tone and beautify the skin.

Oriental Toilet Water

An exotic and aromatic toilet water that will tantalise your senses. Splash it on your body after a shower or bath to leave your skin feeling fragrant and refreshed.

6 TABLESPOONS CHOPPED ANGELICA LEAVES AND STALKS

6 TABLESPOONS CHOPPED LEMON BALM LEAVES

15 G (½ OZ) CORIANDER SEEDS, CRUSHED

1 NUTMEG, GRATED

2 TABLESPOONS CLOVES

4 X 25 MM (1 IN) STICKS OF CINNAMON

300 ML (10 FL OZ) VODKA

Put the herbs and spices in a large, wide-mouthed glass jar, add the vodka, seal and shake vigorously. Leave in a warm place for 3 weeks, shaking every day. Strain through fine muslin and then drip through filter paper into a pretty glass bottle. If you have any, use those with airtight ground glass stoppers—they look attractive on bathroom vanities or bedroom dressing tables.

Orange-Scented Bath Oil

Aromatic oils in your bath water will not only leave your skin smelling wonderfully fragrant and feeling silky-textured, they will also fill the whole bathroom with stimulating scented steam. The spicy scent of this citrus combination will energise your body and lift your senses.

15 ML (½ FL OZ) LEMON OIL
30 ML (1 FL OZ) ORANGE OIL
1 TEASPOON LIME OIL
65 ML (2 FL OZ) ALMOND OIL

Put the almond oil in an amber-coloured glass bottle, add the essential oils, seal and shake well. Leave for 2 weeks so the final scent will mature.

Add 15 to 20 ml (½ to ⅔ fl oz) of oil to a bath of hot water. Shake well before each use.

SPICY

Perfumed Beads

These spicy beads are made from a delightful mixture of exotic spices and gums. They may be strung on fine strong thread and worn as necklaces or earrings. Perfumed beads make wonderful gifts: whoever wears them will be continually enticed by their provocative fragrance—the warmer the wearer gets, the stronger the scent becomes.

30 G (1 OZ) GUM BENZOIN, POWDERED
30 G (1 OZ) GUM ARABIC, POWDERED
15 G (½ OZ) POWDERED ORRIS ROOT
15 G (½ OZ) POWDERED CINNAMON
15 G (½ OZ) POWDERED CLOVE
2 DROPS PURE VANILLA ESSENCE
½ TEASPOON NUTMEG, GRATED
30 ML (1 FL OZ) GLYCERINE
10 ML (⅓ FL OZ) ESSENTIAL OIL OF ROSE

Mix all the ingredients thoroughly, adding the essential oil last, until you have a paste. Form mixture into small balls the size of a pea and spread out on a tray to dry. When dry enough to handle pierce a hole through each one. Spread beads out on a baking tray and place in cool oven until thoroughly dry. String onto strong thread for necklaces or hang from earrings.

Experiment with your choice of essential oils, either singly or in combination, to create your own unique fragrance. For instance, to set a particular mood try replacing the essential oil of rose with any of the following:

RELAXING	STIMULATING	ROMANTIC
SANDALWOOD	MELISSA	PATCHOULI
GERANIUM	CARDAMOM	JASMINE
FRANKINCENSE	ORANGE	ROSE
CLARY-SAGE	BLACK PEPPER	YLANG YLANG

Bath Vinegar

SCENTED VINEGARS ARE REFRESHING AND INVIGORATING. WHEN ADDED TO A HOT BATH THEY WILL ACT AS AN ASTRINGENT AND HAVE A NOTICEABLE SOFTENING EFFECT ON THE SKIN.

This spearmint-scented bath vinegar is especially invigorating, with a revitalising and satisfying scent that clears the head and improves breathing. Add it to a hot bath for a patient suffering from a cold or 'flu.

Mint Bath Vinegar

3 TABLESPOONS FRESHLY CHOPPED SPEARMINT, OR 1 TABLESPOON DRIED SPEARMINT
250 ML (8 FL OZ) CIDER VINEGAR
250 ML (8 FL OZ) DISTILLED WATER

Mix the vinegar and distilled water in an enamel pan and heat until boiling. Remove from heat, add the herbs, cover and leave to steep overnight. Strain through fine muslin, squeezing all liquid from the herbs, and bottle.

Add 1 cup (250 ml/8 fl oz) to each bath.

F R A G R A N T   B E A U T Y

Citrus Face Cream

Facial wrinkles cannot be permanently eliminated, but they can certainly be smoothed out. Keep your skin soft, supple and youthful-looking with this easy-to-make, fresh-scented cream. Apply to face and neck daily after cleansing and toning, using gentle upward and outward movements.

15 G (½ OZ) BEESWAX
55 ML (2 FL OZ) ALMOND OIL
1 TEASPOON AVOCADO OIL
1 TEASPOON WHEATGERM OIL
20 ML (⅔ FL OZ) DISTILLED WATER
20 ML (⅔ FL OZ) ALOE VERA JUICE
6 DROPS TINCTURE OF BENZOIN
15 DROPS LEMON OIL

Melt the wax in a double pan over a medium heat. When completely liquid add prewarmed base oils, distilled water and aloe vera juice, stirring until well blended.

Remove from heat and pour into a ceramic bowl. Add remaining ingredients and beat until cool and creamy. Store in a sterilised glass jar with a tight-fitting lid.

Aphrodisiac Massage Oil

Essential oils have been used as aphrodisiacs ever since romance has been recorded. What better way to show your appreciation of your partner than by giving a romantic and sensuous massage?

30 ML (1 FL OZ) OF JOJOBA OIL
10 DROPS JASMINE ESSENTIAL OIL
10 DROPS MANDARIN ESSENTIAL OIL
5 DROPS BLACK PEPPER ESSENTIAL OIL
5 DROPS NUTMEG ESSENTIAL OIL

Seal all ingredients in a jar, cap securely and shake well. Ideally, a massage oil should be warmed to room temperature before use, to enhance its relaxing effect.

If, however, all that is on your mind is sharing an aromatic bath and then going to bed. . . well, 3 drops of ylang ylang oil and 2 drops of rose oil added to a warm bath will set the mood.

Smelling Salts

ZESTY SMELLING SALTS AND VINAIGRETTES MAKE A
USEFUL ADDITION TO THE BATHROOM VANITY CABINET
OR CUPBOARD. HOLD THEM UNDER YOUR NOSE TO
RELIEVE A STUFFY NOSE OR HEADACHE.

Smelling Salts

Fill a small amber-coloured bottle with coarse sea salt.
Add 1 teaspoon tincture of benzoin and 1 teaspoon of
mandarin, tangerine, orange or lemon essential oil.

Vinaigrette

A vinaigrette is no more than a strong-scented herbal vinegar, usually kept in a special 'smelling bottle'. They were extremely popular in Regency England, being considered an essential accessory for fashionable young men and women meeting in crowded ballrooms and stuffy taverns.

150 ML (5 FL OZ) CIDER VINEGAR
150 ML (5 FL OZ) DISTILLED WATER
2 TABLESPOONS DRIED LAVENDER
2 TABLESPOONS DRIED ROSEMARY
1 TABLESPOON DRIED MINT
1 TABLESPOON DRIED MARJORAM
1 TEASPOON CAMPHORATED OIL

Put all the herbs in a ceramic bowl. Mix together the cider vinegar and distilled water, and heat in an enamel pan to just below boiling point. Pour the liquid over the herbs, cover tightly with plastic cling wrap and leave to steep for 24 hours. Strain, add the camphorated oil and mix well.

Push a small piece of natural sponge into a bottle. Pour in the vinegar liquid and seal tightly. Any leftover liquid can be bottled and given to friends as a gift.

To use, remove the lid and hold the bottle under your nose. Breathe deeply to revive yourself if you are feeling faint, or to clear a stuffed-up nose.

Sandalwood Face Mask

A soothing face mask suitable for all skin types.
The natural yoghurt and Fuller's earth will thoroughly
cleanse facial skin, removing all traces of grease, grime
and stale make-up. The essential oils and honey will
soften and scent the skin, leaving your face feeling
refreshed.

½ CUP (125 ML/4 FL OZ) PLAIN YOGHURT
½ TEASPOON FULLER'S EARTH
½ TEASPOON UNPROCESSED HONEY
2 DROPS SANDALWOOD OIL
2 DROPS ALMOND OIL

SPICY

Blend all ingredients, ensuring that they are thoroughly
mixed together. Apply mask to face and neck,
avoiding the eyes. Lie back and relax for 10 to 15
minutes while the mask cleanses and tones your skin.
Rinse off with tepid water and moisturise.

This face mask is ideal for people who suffer from
acne or other skin disorders, as it will help to destroy
bacteria as well as having a soothing and calming effect
on reddened or sensitive skin.

Herbal Aftershave Lotion

1 ½ TABLESPOONS CHOPPED SAGE LEAVES
1 ½ TABLESPOONS ROSEMARY
1 ½ CUPS (375 ML/12 FL OZ) CIDER VINEGAR
1 ½ CUPS (375 ML/12 FL OZ) WITCH HAZEL
(FROM THE CHEMIST)

Put the herbs in a large, wide-mouthed glass jar. Gently warm the cider vinegar, pour into the jar, seal tightly, and leave where it will receive plenty of hot sun for 2 weeks. Shake the contents every day. Strain, stir in witch hazel and drip through filter paper. Store in a glass bottle and cap securely with a non-metallic lid.

If the scent is not strong enough, repeat the process by adding a fresh batch of herbs to the vinegar.

AN ANGUS & ROBERTSON PUBLICATION

ANGUS&ROBERTSON, AN IMPRINT OF
HARPERCOLLINS*PUBLISHERS*
25 RYDE ROAD, PYMBLE, SYDNEY NSW 2073, AUSTRALIA
31 VIEW ROAD, GLENFIELD, AUCKLAND 10, NEW ZEALAND
77—85 FULHAM PALACE ROAD, LONDON W6 8JB, UNITED KINGDOM
10 EAST 53RD STREET, NEW YORK NY 10022, USA

FIRST PUBLISHED IN AUSTRALIA IN 1995

NATIONAL LIBRARY OF AUSTRALIA
CATALOGUING-IN-PUBLICATION DATA:

HAYES, ALAN B. (ALAN BRUCE), 1949-.
SPICY.
ISBN 0 207 18228 0.
1. NATURE CRAFT. POTPOURRIS (SCENTED FLORAL MIXTURES).
3. SPICES. 4. HERBAL COSMETICS. I. TITLE.

745.5

DESIGN BY LIZ SEYMOUR
ILLUSTRATIONS BY STEVEN BRAY
PRINTED IN HONG KONG

9 8 7 6 5 4 3 2 1
98 97 96 95